TWINKLE TWINKLE LITTLE STAR

Published in the UK by Scholastic, 2024
1 London Bridge, London, SE1 9BG
Scholastic Ireland, 89E Lagan Road, Dublin Industrial
Estate, Glasnevin, Dublin, D11 HP5F

SCHOLASTIC and associated logos are trademarks and/or
registered trademarks of Scholastic Inc.

Text © Scholastic, 2024
Illustrations by Lucy Rogers © Scholastic, 2024
Cover by Lucy Rogers © Scholastic, 2024

ISBN 978 0702 32542 7

A CIP catalogue record for this book is available from the British Library.

All rights reserved.
This book is sold subject to the condition that it shall not, by way of trade
or otherwise, be lent, hired out or otherwise circulated in any form of
binding or cover other than that in which it is published. No part of this
publication may be reproduced, stored in a retrieval system, or transmitted
in any form or by any other means (electronic, mechanical, photocopying,
recording or otherwise) without prior written permission of Scholastic Limited.

Printed in China by C&C Offset Printing Co., Ltd.
Paper made from wood grown in sustainable
forests and other controlled sources.

1 3 5 7 9 10 8 6 4 2

www.scholastic.co.uk

TWINKLE TWINKLE LITTLE STAR

LUCY ROGERS

How I wonder: hook your index finger into the shape of a question mark and circle it to the side of your head

what you are: point your index finger up and wave your hand back and forth

Up above: point your index finger up and raise your hand

the world so high: make a circle shape with your hands

Like a diamond: make a diamond shape with your thumbs and index fingers

in the sky: raise your diamond shape up towards the sky

Twinkle, twinkle: flutter your fingers, moving your hands back and forth

little star: flick your middle finger against your thumb

How I wonder: hook your index finger into the shape of a question mark and circle it to the side of your head

what you are: point your index finger up and wave your hand back and forth

Twinkle, twinkle,

little star,

How I wonder ...

what you are!

Up above ...

the world so high,

Like a diamond ...

in the sky.

little star,

How I wonder

what you are!

Want to find out more?

One of the best ways to learn sign language is to start with the alphabet. Can you learn how to sign your name? What about the name of your best friend? Or your pet?

Sometimes, when you watch TV, you may have noticed someone signing in the corner of the screen. Watch their actions closely. Can you match their actions to the words you hear?

There are some wonderful resources online, including videos on popular streaming channels and apps. Watch some videos to learn how to sign-along to new songs. You could also ask your Deaf friends and family members to teach you.

Be patient. It can take a long time to learn a new language, so start small. Maybe you could learn the sign to one new word every day?

Why not take this book into your school or nursery? Your whole class can then sign along to Twinkle Twinkle!